SAINSBURY'S

Quick and Easy

Curries

Azmina Govindji

2½p
3

Contents

Published exclusively for J Sainsbury plc
Stamford House Stamford Street
London SE1 9LL

by Martin Books
Simon & Schuster Consumer Group
Grafton House 64 Maids Causeway
Cambridge CB5 8DD

First published September 1994
Third impression November 1995

ISBN 0 85941 864 2

Printed and bound in the UK by Bath Press Colourbooks
Design: Green Moore Lowenhoff
Photography: Iain Bagwell
Styling: Maria Kelly
Food preparation: Berit Vinegrad
Typesetting: Goodfellow & Egan Ltd, Cambridge

Pictured on the front cover: Fish Curry (page 32)

Introduction

The great Indian take-away and pre-cooked Asian meals are rising in popularity. Exposure to such exotic tastes has no doubt led to an increased desire for people to prepare unusual and exciting meals at home. Juggling a demanding job with a husband, two toddlers and housework has certainly pushed me into learning how to conjure up an aromatic Indian dish in about half an hour. So, if you lead a hectic life or simply fancy a curry in a hurry, these recipes will give you delicious and authentic flavours in minutes. All recipes are original and have been tried and tested.

Being of Indian origin, and having lived in the UK, I have always been keen to mix east and west. Recipes such as Salmon in Coriander and Almond Sauce (page 34) offer a perfect combination of the two. Children have also been catered for. My toddlers, Bizhan and Shazia, are being exposed to traditional Indian cooking at home in the way of 'finger foods', such as Chilli and Herb Chicken Wings (page 6) and Seekh Kebabs (page 8).

Most of the dishes are nutritious, too, incorporating lentils, lean minced meat and fish, and using oils rather than butter for frying. I particularly recommend rapeseed oil, which is sold in Sainsbury's as 'vegetable oil'. Choose lean cuts of meat and skinless poultry for delicious, low-fat Indian-style dishes.

SPECIAL INGREDIENTS

Listed below are some basic spices which are the essence of Indian cooking. This list may look daunting, but you will find these spices used frequently: investing in them will give you the opportunity to try lots of recipes.

Caraway seeds A pungently flavoured spice, good with vegetables and in sauces.

Cardamom pods These are used in pilaus and meat dishes to add aroma. Remember to warn the family not to eat them.

Chillies, green The quantity suggested in these recipes will make a mild to medium dish. Adjust this to suit your individual taste. Take great care when preparing chillies as the juice can sting eyes and nose if you touch them. Wearing rubber gloves and handling chillies under running water can help. Chillies lose some of their heat if de-seeded.

Chilli powder This is available in mild, medium and hot varieties.

Cinnamon An aromatic stick which imparts more essence and flavour when broken up.

Cloves Whole cloves are generally used in pilau and meat dishes to provide a characteristic aroma.

Coriander A green leafy herb, which is used extensively in Asian cooking and as a garnish. Whole coriander seeds impart a different flavour to cooked dishes.

Ground coriander seeds are often combined with ground cumin seeds and used as a *masala* (spice) base for curry.

Crispy topping onions Not a spice, but a ready-made product that makes an excellent quick substitute for deep-fried onions. These are often used in Indian dishes to add depth of flavour to sauces, and as a garnish.

Cumin Cumin seeds are often fried in oil to release a rich distinctive aroma; they burn easily. Ground cumin is used in spice bases.

Curry leaves A fragrant herb that resembles bay leaves, these are used mainly in dhal dishes.

Dill pepper As the name suggests, a blend of peppercorns and dill seeds.

Fennel seeds An aniseed-flavoured spice, often fried in oil in the first stage of cooking, to make full use of its aromatic quality.

Fenugreek seeds Fenugreek seeds have a distinctive and pungent aroma and flavour, which is released when the seeds are fried. Ground fenugreek is used in spice bases.

Garlic-grain pepper A garlic-flavoured blend of peppercorns.

Garam masala A combination of ground spices.

Garlic These recipes use quick-frozen garlic, which I feel is the closest you will get to the freshly puréed version. Adjust amounts according to your personal preference.

Ginger These recipes incorporate freeze-dried ginger which, in my opinion, has a stronger flavour than fresh ginger. If you prefer fresh ginger, use twice the suggested quantities.

Mustard seeds, black Tiny seeds that are fried to allow the fragrance to escape.

Paprika A red ground spice with a sweet flavour, used mainly for garnishing.

Poppy seeds Very hard seeds that are dry-roasted and fried at the beginning of recipes to release their flavour.

Sesame seeds Light-coloured seeds with a delicious, nutty flavour.

Tandoori spice mix A ready-prepared mixture of spices to give instant 'tandoori' flavour.

Tamarind A piquant fruit which gives a characteristic sharp taste, something like lemon juice. These recipes use a ready-made pickle containing tamarind, to capture its unique flavour.

Turmeric A ground spice that gives a wonderful yellow colour and a distinctive flavour to all kinds of curries.

COOKING TIPS

* When mustard seeds are fried, they can pop and jump out of the pan! Protect yourself by covering the pan and lowering the heat.

* Mustard and cumin seeds can burn very quickly and become bitter. Be particularly careful with cumin seeds. Some recipes suggest you remove the pan from the heat until the cumin seeds stop crackling.

* Yogurt often curdles when used in cooking. I do not worry if this happens, but you can lessen the effect by beating the yogurt with a teaspoon of cornflour first, and adding it a little at a time. Stir continuously till the yogurt heats through and make sure it doesn't boil.

* The flavour of Indian cooking develops if water is added at intervals rather than all at once.

* Use strong non-stick cookware with tight-fitting lids so that the aroma and steam have less chance to escape.

* Try to avoid using light-coloured plastic utensils in cooking, since these may become slightly discoloured by turmeric. Wipe up any spills on work-surfaces or the floor, to avoid staining.

ACKNOWLEDGEMENTS

I would like to thank the following people for their assistance in the preparation of this book: Aarti Dattani, Malek Govindji, Mary Lakhani, Nabat Virani, Moez Jaffer and Nazma Lakhani; my mother, Roshan Noormohamed for providing me with a strong tradition of Indian cooking; Nazira Jaffer for typing the manuscript and Jill Oneill for her honest comments on tasting. But most of all, my deepest appreciation must go to my husband, Shamil, whose tolerance and support have enabled me to channel much of my energy into this book.

RECIPE NOTES

All recipes in this book give ingredients in both metric (g, ml, etc.) and Imperial (oz, pints, etc.) measures. Use either set of quantities, but not a mixture of both, in any one recipe.

All teaspoons and tablespoons are level, unless otherwise stated. 1 teaspoon = a 5 ml spoon; 1 tablespoon = a 15 ml spoon.

Egg size is medium (size 3), unless otherwise stated.

Vegetables and fruit are medium-size unless otherwise stated.

Freshly ground black pepper should be used throughout.

PREPARATION AND COOKING TIMES

Preparation and cooking times are included at the head of the recipes as a general guide; preparation times, especially, are approximate and timings are usually rounded to the nearest 5 minutes.

Preparation times include the time taken to prepare ingredients in the list, but not to make any 'basic' recipe.

The cooking times given at the heads of the recipes denote cooking periods when the dish can be left largely unattended, e.g. baking, and not the total amount of cooking for the recipe. Always read and follow the timings given for the steps of the recipe in the method.

Light Meals

Indian-style dishes make great 'finger foods' that can be prepared very quickly. Quick-cooking cuts of meat and fresh vegetables are given instant appetite-appeal with spicy coatings, marinades and sauces.

Chilli and Herb Chicken Wings

Preparation and cooking time: 25 minutes.
Freezing: recommended at the end of step 2. Serves 3–4.

An easy and economical meal, which goes well with salad and garlic bread or naan bread. I often serve it with Chilli Chips (page 78) for my children who love such 'finger foods'.

750 g (1½ lb) chicken wings
For the sauce:
2½ tablespoons olive oil
2 teaspoons dried oregano
2 teaspoons dried dill

2 teaspoons garlic purée
2 fresh green chillies, chopped very finely
1 tablespoon chilli sauce
1 teaspoon salt, or to taste

❶ Preheat the grill to medium-hot. Line a large flameproof dish with foil.
❷ Mix the sauce ingredients together and pour this over the chicken wings, making sure that the wings have been evenly coated.

❸ Put the wings into the dish and grill for 20–25 minutes, turning and basting them frequently. Serve immediately.

Spicy Corn on the Cob

Preparation and cooking time: 30 minutes.
Freezing: not recommended. Serves 4.

8 frozen mini corn on the cobs

3 tablespoons vegetable or corn oil

½ teaspoon black mustard seeds

1 teaspoon cumin seeds

3 curry leaves

2 onions, chopped finely

1 teaspoon quick-frozen garlic

2 fresh green chillies, chopped very
   finely

1 teaspoon ground turmeric

½ teaspoon salt, or to taste

½ teaspoon ground cumin

250 g (8 oz) passata (sieved tomatoes)

½ teaspoon garam masala

1 tablespoon lemon juice

15 g packet of fresh coriander, chopped, to
   garnish

❶ Cook the corn on the cob until tender.

❷ Heat the oil and add the mustard seeds. Cover and allow to pop for a few seconds.

❸ Add the cumin seeds, curry leaves, onions, garlic and chillies and fry for 2–3 minutes.

❹ Add the turmeric, salt, cumin and passata. Stir well. Add the cooked corn on the cob, garam masala and lemon juice. Simmer for 5 minutes.

❺ Garnish and serve hot or cold.

Seekh Kebabs

Preparation and cooking time: 25 minutes.
Freezing: recommended after step 4. Makes 12 kebabs.

2 slices of bread, crusts removed

500 g (1 lb) lean minced lamb

1 teaspoon quick-frozen garlic

½ teaspoon freeze-dried ginger

2–3 fresh green chillies, chopped very finely

1 teaspoon chilli powder

1 teaspoon salt, or to taste

½ teaspoon garlic-grain pepper (optional)

1 small onion, grated

15 g packet of fresh coriander, chopped
   finely

3 teaspoons garam masala

2 teaspoons Worcestershire sauce

1 egg, beaten

tomato quarters, to garnish

❶ Preheat the grill and line the grill pan with aluminium foil.

❷ Wet the bread under a running tap and squeeze out excess water.

❸ Add the bread to all the other ingredients and mix well.

❹ Shape the spiced minced meat into sausages and thread them on metal skewers if you like (this speeds up the cooking). Place the kebabs directly on the grill pan.

❺ Cook under the hot grill for around 15 minutes, turning to ensure even cooking.

❻ Garnish and serve hot.

Boti Kebabs

Preparation and cooking time: 40 minutes.
Freezing: not recommended.
Makes 10–12 × 20 cm (8-inch) skewers.

A colourful beef kebab dish that can also be made with cubed chicken or white fish. You will need small wooden skewers and, if you shallow-fry these kebabs, a large non-stick frying-pan with a lid. You can also cook the kebabs under a hot grill, in which case, line the grill pan with aluminium foil and place the skewers directly on this foil. Serve on a bed of lettuce, with warmed pitta bread and salad.

875 g (1¾ lb) rump steak, cut into 2.5
   cm (1-inch) cubes
175 g (6 oz) button mushrooms
4 tomatoes, quartered
1 large green pepper, de-seeded and cut
   into 2.5 cm (1-inch) squares
curry powder
oil for shallow-frying or drizzling

For the sauce:
½–1 teaspoon salt, or to taste
2 tablespoons lemon juice
2 fresh green chillies, chopped very
   finely
½ teaspoon freeze-dried ginger
½ teaspoon quick-frozen garlic
2 tablespoons chilli and garlic sauce
1 tablespoon garam masala

❶ Preheat the grill, if using.
❷ Make the sauce by mixing all the ingredients together. Mix this well with the meat.
❸ Thread pieces of meat and vegetables alternately on to the skewers.
❹ Sprinkle curry powder liberally over the prepared kebabs. Drizzle with oil if using the grill.
❺ Shallow-fry or grill the kebabs, turning frequently with tongs, for about 20 minutes.
❻ Drain on kitchen paper and serve immediately.

Spiced-Chicken Pitta Pockets

Preparation time: 10 minutes + 20 minutes cooking.
Freezing: recommended after step 4. Serves 4.

2 tablespoons olive oil

3 boneless, skinless chicken breasts, cut
into thin strips

1½ teaspoons quick-frozen garlic

1 teaspoon freeze-dried ginger

2 fresh green chillies, chopped very
    finely

½ teaspoon salt, or to taste

1 tablespoon lemon juice

1 teaspoon ground cumin

1 teaspoon ground coriander

100 ml (3½ fl oz) hot water

4 spring onions, chopped finely

15 g packet of fresh coriander, chopped

2 teaspoons garam masala

pepper and chilli sauce, to taste

To serve:

4 pitta breads, halved

shredded lettuce

cubed cucumber

❶ Heat the oil in a large non-stick frying-pan or wok with a lid. Gently fry the chicken over a medium heat for 3 minutes.

❷ Add the garlic, ginger, chillies, salt, lemon juice, ground cumin, ground coriander and water. Season with black pepper and chilli sauce to taste.

❸ Cover and cook for 20 minutes, stirring occasionally.

❹ Add the spring onions, chopped fresh coriander and garam masala. Stir well.

❺ Warm the halved pitta breads in a low oven. Fill the pitta-bread 'pockets' with lettuce, cucumber and, lastly, the spiced chicken. Serve immediately.

Courgette Curry

Preparation and cooking time: 25 minutes.
Freezing: recommended. Serves 4–6.

2 tablespoons vegetable or corn oil

1 heaped teaspoon black mustard seeds

½ teaspoon fennel seeds

1.25 kg (3 lb) courgettes, cubed

2–3 fresh green chillies, chopped very finely

1 teaspoon freeze-dried ginger

1 teaspoon quick-frozen garlic

175 g (6 oz) canned chopped tomatoes

1 teaspoon salt

1 teaspoon ground mixed spice (optional)

½ teaspoon ground turmeric

½ teaspoon ground coriander

½ teaspoon ground cumin

½ teaspoon chilli powder, or to taste

To serve:

1 teaspoon garam masala

15 g packet of fresh coriander, chopped

❶ Heat the oil in a saucepan over a medium heat. Add the mustard seeds, cover the pan and allow the seeds to pop for a few seconds.

❷ Stir in the fennel seeds and courgettes and fry gently for 3 minutes.

❸ Add all the other ingredients, and stir well.

❹ Cover, and cook for 5 minutes or until the courgettes are just tender.

❺ Add the garam masala and chopped fresh coriander and serve hot.

Tandoori Prawns

Preparation time: 10 minutes + 10 minutes cooking.
Freezing: not recommended. Serves 2–3.

1 tablespoon olive oil
1 onion, chopped finely
5 cm (2-inch) cinnamon stick, broken
½ teaspoon quick-frozen garlic
1–2 fresh green chillies, chopped very finely
200 g (7 oz) frozen peeled prawns
1 teaspoon garam masala
15 g packet of fresh coriander, chopped finely

For the tandoori sauce:
3 teaspoons tandoori spice mix
½ teaspoon salt
250 g (8 oz) natural yogurt
125 g (4 oz) passata (sieved tomatoes)
1 spring onion, sliced finely, to garnish

❶ Heat the oil and fry the onion, cinnamon pieces, garlic and chillies for 2–3 minutes.
❷ Add the prawns and fry gently for 3 minutes.
❸ Meanwhile, mix the sauce ingredients together. Add the sauce to the prawns and stir well.
❹ Cook, uncovered, for 10 minutes, stirring occasionally.
❺ Add the garam masala and chopped fresh coriander and stir. Garnish and serve at once.

Egg-Fried Bread

Preparation and cooking time: 15 minutes.
Freezing: not recommended. Serves 2.

3 eggs, beaten
1 fresh green chilli, chopped very finely
¼ teaspoon salt, or to taste
½ teaspoon coarsely ground black pepper, or to taste

15 g packet of fresh coriander, chopped finely
chilli powder (optional)
oil for shallow-frying
4 slices of bread, halved diagonally

❶ Combine the beaten egg with the chilli, salt, pepper, chopped fresh coriander and chilli powder (if used). Mix thoroughly.
❷ Heat the oil in a frying-pan. Dip each triangle of bread into the spiced egg and shallow-fry until golden brown on both sides.
❸ Drain on kitchen paper and serve immediately.

Meat and Fish Main Courses

Indian-style dishes can make quick and easy main courses if you choose lean, quick-cooking cuts of meat such as boneless chicken, and ready-prepared fish fillets. The following recipes may have quite long lists of ingredients, but there is really very little preparation involved – just add your spices and let them work their magic as they cook.

Chicken Thighs with Poppy Seeds

Preparation time: 20 minutes + 35 minutes cooking.
Freezing: recommended. Serves 5.

Indian cooking usually requires the chicken to be skinned. You can buy skinless thighs, but I find skinning them at home is quite easy and more economical. Serve this with naan bread and a crisp green salad.

3 tablespoons vegetable or corn oil	3 tablespoons crispy topping onions
2–3 fresh green chillies, chopped very finely	10 chicken thighs on the bone, skinned
2 teaspoons freeze-dried ginger	1 tablespoon coriander seeds
3 teaspoons garlic purée	1 tablespoon poppy seeds
1½ teaspoons chilli powder	1½ tablespoons sesame seeds
1½ teaspoons salt, or to taste	2 tablespoons ground almonds
1 teaspoon ground turmeric	1 teaspoon garam masala
1 teaspoon ground coriander	2 × 15 g packet of fresh coriander, chopped roughly
1 teaspoon ground cumin	
230 g can of chopped tomatoes	toasted flaked almonds, to garnish

❶ Heat the oil over a low heat and stir-fry the chillies, ginger and garlic purée for 1 minute.

❷ Add the chilli powder, salt, turmeric, coriander and cumin, and stir-fry for a further minute.

❸ Add the tomatoes and crispy topping onions. Stir, and simmer for 3 minutes.

❹ Add the chicken and fry gently over a medium heat for 10 minutes.

❺ Meanwhile, dry-roast the coriander, poppy and sesame seeds in a small pan over a low heat for 1 minute. Stir frequently.

❻ Allow the seeds to cool, and then partially grind them in a coffee grinder or by placing them in a polythene bag and crushing them with a rolling pin.

❼ Add the dry-roasted ingredients and the ground almonds to the chicken. Stir well, cover and cook for 35 minutes, or until the chicken is thoroughly cooked.

❽ Add the garam masala and chopped fresh coriander and stir until these are fully dispersed.

❾ Garnish and serve

Tandoori Chicken

Preparation and cooking time: marinating (optional) + 30 minutes. Freezing: recommended after step 2. Serves 6.

Tandoor cooking is traditionally carried out in a very hot clay oven. The food is cooked quickly and the finished product is often slightly charred. The flavour of this recipe is improved if the chicken is marinated beforehand, but it is not essential. Try this with warm pitta bread and a green salad.

1.75 kg (4 lb) chicken or 10 skinless,
   boneless chicken thighs, cut into small pieces

For the sauce:

2 × 150 g (5 oz) carton of natural yogurt

2 tablespoons tomato purée

½ teaspoon quick-frozen garlic

½ teaspoon freeze-dried ginger

chilli powder, to taste

1 teaspoon Kashmiri masala (optional)

2 tablespoons soy sauce

2 tablespoons Worcestershire sauce

1 tablespoon vinegar

4 tablespoons vegetable or corn oil

2 teaspoons salt, or to taste

2 teaspoons tandoori spice mix

1 teaspoon ground cumin

❶ Mix all the sauce ingredients together.

❷ Pour this marinade over the chicken pieces and stir until the chicken is completely coated.

❸ Marinate for 2 hours, if time permits.

❹ Preheat the grill. Place the chicken in a shallow roasting tin lined with aluminium foil.

❺ Cook the chicken under a hot grill for 20 minutes, turning and basting frequently.

Jeera Chicken

Preparation time: 20 minutes + 10 minutes cooking.
Freezing: recommended. Serves 4–6.

A favourite in most households and Indian restaurants, this distinctly flavoured dish (the name means 'cumin') is usually served with a border of Jeera Potatoes (page 70) and naan bread. Use a non-stick wok, if you have one.

3 teaspoons coriander seeds
4 tablespoons olive oil
2 teaspoons cumin seeds
2 onions, sliced finely
3 fresh green chillies, chopped very finely
1½ teaspoons quick-frozen garlic
½ teaspoon freeze-dried ginger

6 boneless, skinless chicken breasts, cut into
  2.5 cm (1-inch) chunks
1 teaspoon ground turmeric
1 heaped teaspoon salt, or to taste
1 teaspoon ground cumin
1½ teaspoons garam masala
3 × 15 g packet of fresh coriander
2 tablespoons lemon juice

❶ Partially grind the coriander seeds in a coffee grinder, or by placing them in a polythene bag and crushing them with a rolling pin.
❷ Heat the oil in a non-stick wok. Add the cumin seeds and onions. Fry gently for 2–3 minutes.
❸ Add the chillies, garlic and ginger and stir well.
❹ Add the chicken, turmeric and salt. Fry gently for 5 minutes until the chicken turns a yellowish colour.

❺ Add the cumin, partially ground coriander seeds and garam masala.
❻ Cover and cook over a medium heat for 10 minutes, stirring occasionally.
❼ Reserve a few sprigs of fresh coriander to garnish and finely chop the rest. Add the lemon juice and chopped fresh coriander to the wok and stir well. Serve at once.

Eastern Fried Chicken

Preparation and cooking time: 35 minutes.
Freezing: not recommended. Serves 4.

A perfect combination of east and west that goes well with Chilli Chips (page 78), salad and Tamarind Sauce (page 74). It takes advantage of a ready-made Indian-style coating mix, to which I often add chilli powder for a bit of extra zing – try it if you dare! You will find that the breadcrumbs do disperse a little into the oil: strain this flavoured oil and reuse it for other Indian cooking.

2 fresh green chillies, chopped very finely

2 teaspoons quick-frozen garlic

½ teaspoon freeze-dried ginger

1 teaspoon salt, or to taste

15 g packet of fresh coriander, chopped finely

8 chicken drumsticks

6 tablespoon water

1 teaspoon chilli powder (optional)

70 g packet of crispy crumb Indian coating mix

1 egg, beaten

vegetable or corn oil for deep-frying

❶ Rub the chillies, garlic, ginger, salt and chopped fresh coriander into the chicken drumsticks.

❷ Put the water in a saucepan large enough to take all the drumsticks in one layer. Add the drumsticks and cover with a tight-fitting lid. Cook over a medium heat for 15 minutes.

❸ Remove the drumsticks with a slotted spoon and drain them on kitchen paper.

❹ If adding chilli powder, mix this with the coating mix. Dip the chicken into the beaten egg, and then into the coating mix.

❺ Deep-fry the drumsticks in hot oil till golden brown (around 15 minutes).

Rogan Josh

Preparation time: 15 minutes + 25 minutes cooking.
Freezing: recommended. Serves 4.

The aroma emanating from the whole spices in this dish is so mouthwatering that this is certainly a popular dish in the Govindji family! Serve with rice and a refreshing Cucumber Raita (page 74).

3 tablespoons vegetable oil

1 teaspoon cumin seeds

½ teaspoon fennel seeds

2 cardamom pods

5 cm (2-inch) cinnamon stick, broken

4 cloves

6 black peppercorns

½ teaspoon freeze-dried ginger

1 teaspoon quick-frozen garlic

3 green chillies, chopped very finely

875 g (1¾ lb) rump steak, cut into 2.5 cm (1-inch) cubes

335 g jar of rogan josh cooking sauce

3 tablespoons crispy topping onions

½ teaspoon ground turmeric

1 teaspoon salt, or to taste

150 g (5 oz) carton of natural yogurt, whisked briefly

3 tablespoons chopped almonds

2 × 15 g packet of fresh coriander, chopped

1 teaspoon garam masala

15 g (½ oz) pine kernels, to garnish

❶ Heat the oil in a large, heavy frying-pan. Add the cumin and fennel seeds, cardamoms, cinnamon pieces, cloves and peppercorns.

❷ Stir in the ginger, garlic, chillies and steak. Fry gently over a medium to high heat till the meat has browned.

❸ Add the cooking sauce, crispy topping onions, turmeric and salt. Stir well. Cover and cook over medium heat for 10–15 minutes, stirring occasionally.

❹ Add all the other ingredients. Bring the sauce back to the boil whilst stirring. Cover and simmer for 5–10 minutes until the meat is cooked, stirring occasionally.

Karahi Gosht

Preparation time: 15 minutes + 25 minutes cooking.
Freezing: recommended. Serves 4.

A slightly piquant dish, made with tender chunks of beef in a thick yogurt sauce. It is traditionally cooked in a *karahi*, which resembles a wok; a good saucepan can also be used. The cream is optional, but it does make a richer, even more delicious sauce. Serve this curry with naan bread and Cucumber Raita (page 74).

3 tablespoons vegetable or corn oil

875 g (1¾ lb) rump steak, cut into small
   chunks

3 teaspoons cumin seeds

2 × 5 cm (2-inch) cinnamon stick, broken

1½ teaspoons garlic purée

1½ teaspoons freeze-dried ginger

3 fresh green chillies, chopped very finely

1 teaspoon paprika

1 teaspoon ground turmeric

1 teaspoon garam masala

1½ teaspoons salt, or to taste

3 teaspoons tomato purée

450 g (14 oz) carton of natural yogurt

2 tomatoes, quartered

15 g packet of fresh coriander, chopped

142 ml (5 fl oz) carton of single cream
   (optional)

❶ Heat 1 tablespoon of oil in a wok or large pan with a tight-fitting lid and brown the steak to seal in the juices.

❷ Meanwhile, partially grind the cumin seeds in a coffee grinder, or alternatively, place the seeds in a polythene bag and crush them using a rolling pin.

❸ Remove the meat and juices from the pan and set aside.

❹ Heat the remaining 2 tablespoons of oil in the pan. Remove from the heat and add the cumin seeds and cinnamon pieces. Allow the seeds to crackle for a few seconds.

❺ Return to the heat and add the garlic

purée, ginger, chillies, paprika, turmeric, garam masala and salt. Fry for 1 minute or until blended, over a low heat.

❻ Add the tomato purée and yogurt. Cook over a medium heat, whilst stirring for 3–5 minutes. The yogurt may curdle, but this is normal.

❼ Add the meat with its juices, cover and cook for 20 minutes or until the meat is tender. Check half-way through cooking, and add a few tablespoons of water if the meat is starting to stick to the bottom of the pan.

❽ Add the tomatoes, cream (if using) and coriander and simmer for 1 minute.

Lamb Cutlets in Thick Tomato Masala

Preparation and cooking time: 30 minutes.
Freezing: Recommended. Serves 4.

8 'tenderlean' lamb cutlets

For the grilling sauce:

2 teaspoons quick-frozen garlic

2 fresh green chillies, chopped very finely

1 teaspoon chilli powder (optional)

½ teaspoon freeze-dried ginger

2 heaped teaspoons tomato purée

1 teaspoon salt, or to taste

For the masala:

3 tablespoons vegetable or corn oil

2 × 5 cm (2-inch) cinnamon stick, broken

2 teaspoons ground cumin

250 g (8 oz) passata (sieved tomatoes)

2 heaped teaspoons tomato purée

4 tablespoons crispy topping onions

1 teaspoon ground turmeric

2 teaspoons hot curry paste

1 fresh green chilli, chopped very finely

1 teaspoon curry powder

15 g packet of fresh coriander, chopped

salt, to taste

spring onions, cut into 2.5 cm (1-inch)
    diagonal strips, to garnish

❶ Preheat the grill to high and line the grill pan with aluminium foil.

❷ Make the grilling sauce by mixing all the ingredients together. Rub this well into the cutlets.

❸ Grill the cutlets for 15 minutes, basting and turning them occasionally.

❹ Meanwhile, heat the oil for the masala. Add the cinnamon pieces and cumin and immediately stir in the passata.

❺ Add the tomato purée, crispy topping onions, turmeric, curry paste, chilli, curry powder and salt.

❻ Simmer this sauce over a low heat, stirring occasionally, while the lamb cutlets cook.

❼ Add the cutlets and chopped fresh coriander to the masala, cover and simmer for a further 5 minutes. Garnish and serve.

Masala Fish

Preparation time: 30 minutes.
Freezing: recommended. Serves 4–6.

This spicy dish is also delicious when topped with grated cheese and grilled. Serve with Chilli Chips (page 78) or naan bread.

2 large fresh haddock fillets, weighing about
    750 g (1½ lb), each cut into 3
For the paste:
2 fresh green chillies, chopped very finely
½ teaspoon quick-frozen garlic
½ teaspoon freeze-dried ginger
½ teaspoon salt
3 tablespoons lemon juice
2 tablespoons olive oil

For the masala:
4 tablespoons olive oil
300 g (10 oz) passata (sieved tomatoes)
1 heaped tablespoon tomato purée
1 heaped teaspoon chilli powder, or to taste
2 teaspoons ground cumin
1 heaped teaspoon ground coriander
1 teaspoon ground turmeric
½ teaspoon salt, or to taste
125 ml (4 fl oz) hot water
15 g packet of fresh coriander, chopped, to
    garnish

❶ Preheat the grill to medium-hot and line the grill pan with aluminium foil.
❷ Make the paste by mixing all the ingredients together. Coat the fish with this paste and place it on the grill pan.
❸ Cook for 10–15 minutes, turning to ensure even cooking.
❹ Meanwhile, prepare the masala. Heat the oil in a small pan. Add all the other ingredients and stir well.

❺ Cover and cook the masala over a medium heat while the fish cooks fully.
❻ Transfer the grilled fish to a shallow, flameproof serving dish. Cover with the masala.
❼ Return to a hot grill for 5–10 minutes. Garnish and serve.

Fish Curry

Preparation time: 15 minutes + 10 minutes cooking.
Freezing: recommended. Serves 3–4.

3 tablespoons vegetable or sunflower oil

1 large onion, sliced

3 cloves

4 black peppercorns

5 cm (2-inch) cinnamon stick, broken

½ teaspoon quick-frozen garlic

½ teaspoon freeze-dried ginger

2 fresh green chillies, chopped very finely

1 teaspoon ground cumin

1 teaspoon ground coriander

1 teaspoon chilli powder, or to taste

150 g (5 oz) passata (sieved tomatoes)

2 teaspoons tomato purée

1 teaspoon salt, or to taste

1 teaspoon ground turmeric

1 teaspoon hot curry paste (optional)

2 tablespoons crispy topping onions

100 ml (3½ fl oz) hot water

3 large frozen fish fillets, weighing about
    500 g (1 lb), each cut into 3

½ teaspoon garam masala

15 g packet of fresh coriander, chopped

lemon wedges, to garnish

❶ Heat the oil and add the onion, cloves, peppercorns and cinnamon pieces.

❷ Add the garlic, ginger and chillies and fry gently for 2–3 minutes.

❸ Stir in the cumin, coriander and chilli powder. Keep stirring for a few seconds.

❹ Add the passata, tomato purée, salt, turmeric, curry paste (if used), crispy topping onions and water. Stir till the ingredients are well blended.

❺ Drop the fish into the pan, cover and cook over a medium heat till the fish is cooked (about 10 minutes).

❻ Lift the fish out gently using a slotted spoon, and transfer to a serving dish. Add the garam masala and chopped fresh coriander to the remaining sauce and stir.

❼ Pour the sauce over the fish, garnish and serve.

Salmon in Almond and Coriander Sauce

Preparation and cooking time: 25 minutes.
Freezing: not recommended. Serves 4.

A delicately spiced dish that goes well with plain boiled rice, or fresh vegetables and sauté potatoes. This is not a creamy sauce; it is, in fact, quite 'bitty', with crunchy pieces of coriander. An excellent speedy meal for a party menu.

4 salmon steaks

For the grilling sauce:

4 teaspoons herb mustard (optional)

½ teaspoon quick-frozen garlic

1 fresh green chilli, chopped very finely

2–3 tablespoons olive oil, or to taste

1 teaspoon salt, or to taste

1 teaspoon dried basil

1 teaspoon dill pepper (optional)

1 teaspoon dried dill

For the coriander sauce:

2 × 150 g (5 oz) carton of natural yogurt

½ teaspoon ground mixed spice

½ teaspoon ground turmeric

½ teaspoon salt, or to taste

½ teaspoon ground cumin

½ teaspoon ground coriander

1 tablespoon olive oil

½ teaspoon caraway seeds

½ teaspoon cumin seeds

½ teaspoon freeze-dried ginger

½ teaspoon quick-frozen garlic

1 fresh green chilli, chopped very finely

4 tablespoons crispy topping onions

2 × 15 g packet of fresh coriander, chopped

½ teaspoon garam masala

3 tablespoons ground almonds

❶ Preheat the grill to high and line the grill pan with aluminium foil.

❷ Mix all the grilling sauce ingredients together. Coat each salmon steak.

❸ Place the salmon steaks on the grill pan and grill them for 5–7 minutes. Then turn each steak and lower the heat to medium. Cook the other side for about 5 minutes.

❹ Meanwhile, for the coriander sauce, mix together the yogurt, mixed spice, turmeric, salt, cumin and coriander.

❺ Heat the oil in a small frying-pan. Add the caraway and cumin seeds and allow to crackle for a few seconds. Stir in the ginger, garlic and chilli.

❻ Pour the yogurt mixture slowly into the saucepan, whilst stirring. It doesn't matter if it curdles. Add the crispy topping onions and simmer for 5 minutes, stirring frequently.

❼ Add the chopped fresh coriander, garam masala and ground almonds to the saucepan.

❽ Transfer the cooked salmon to a serving dish. Pour the sauce over the fish, leaving part of the steaks uncovered. Serve immediately.

Prawns in Thick Curry Sauce

Preparation and cooking time: 20 minutes.
Freezing: not recommended. Serves 2–3.

This dish is delicious with pitta or naan bread and natural yogurt. However, if you want to serve it with rice, I suggest you add an extra carton of natural yogurt or 100 ml (3 1/2 fl oz) water at step 4.

2 tablespoons vegetable or corn oil

1 onion, chopped

5 cm (2-inch) cinnamon stick, broken

1 teaspoon cumin seeds

1/2 teaspoon quick-frozen garlic

1/2 teaspoon freeze-dried ginger

1 fresh green chilli, chopped very finely

250 g (8 oz) frozen cooked peeled prawns

150 g (5 oz) carton of natural yogurt

1 teaspoon ground turmeric

1/2 teaspoon ground coriander

1/2 teaspoon ground cumin

1/2 teaspoon curry powder

3 tablespoons crispy topping onions

1/2 teaspoon salt, or to taste

1 teaspoon garam masala

1 tablespoon lemon juice

15 g packet of fresh coriander, chopped

❶ Heat the oil in a large non-stick frying-pan. Add the onion and cinnamon pieces and fry gently for 3–5 minutes, until the onion starts to turn brown.

❷ Stir in the cumin seeds.

❸ Add the garlic, ginger, chilli and prawns. Stir-fry for 3–5 minutes.

❹ Meanwhile, mix the yogurt, turmeric, coriander, cumin and curry powder together and beat well.

❺ Remove the prawns and onions from the frying-pan using a slotted spoon, and set aside.

❻ Add the yogurt mixture to the pan, a little at a time, stirring well between additions.

❼ Add the crispy topping onions and salt and allow the ingredients to blend together whilst stirring.

❽ Return the prawns to the pan. Add the garam masala, lemon juice and chopped fresh coriander and cook for a few more minutes.

❾ Serve at once.

creme fraiche?

Vegetarian Main Courses

Vegetable dishes play a very important part in Indian cooking, and not just as accompaniments to meat and fish. These dishes are substantial enough to be main courses on their own, but they are so quick to make you could also combine two or more for a wonderful Indian-style feast.

Potato and Broccoli Curry

Preparation and cooking time: 40 minutes.
Freezing: not recommended. Serves 4.

4 tablespoons vegetable or corn oil

1 teaspoon black mustard seeds

¼ teaspoon fenugreek seeds (optional)

½ teaspoon cumin seeds

1 teaspoon garlic purée

1 teaspoon freeze-dried ginger

2 fresh green chillies, chopped very finely

230 g can of chopped tomatoes

1 teaspoon ground coriander

1 teaspoon ground cumin

1 teaspoon ground turmeric

1½ teaspoons salt, or to taste

750 g (1½ lb) potatoes, peeled and cut into small cubes

200 ml (7 fl oz) hot water

500 g (1 lb) frozen broccoli

15 g packet of fresh coriander, chopped

¼ teaspoon garam masala

❶ Heat the oil over a gentle heat. Add the mustard and fenugreek seeds (if using), cover the pan and allow them to pop for a few seconds.

❷ Remove the pan from the heat and add the cumin seeds. Stir in the garlic purée, ginger, and chillies and return the pan to the heat.

❸ Add the tomatoes, coriander, cumin, turmeric and salt and cook for 3–5 minutes over a medium heat.

❹ Add the potatoes to the pan with 100 ml (3½ fl oz) of the hot water. Cover and cook for 10 minutes.

❺ Add the remaining 100 ml (3½ fl oz) of water, with the broccoli. Cover, and cook for a further 10 minutes.

❻ Stir in the chopped fresh coriander and garam masala and serve.

Red Lentil Dhal with Tarka

Preparation time: 10 minutes soaking + 10 minutes + 20 minutes cooking. Freezing: recommended. Serves 4.

This is a Gujarati dish from western India. 'Tarka' is a method of cooking in which the spice-base is fried in hot oil before being added to the other ingredients. It is traditionally made using *toor dhal* (split pigeon peas), but this recipe uses red lentils, which cook more quickly. Serve with Chapatis (page 72) or plain boiled rice.

250 g (8 oz) red lentils

1½ litres (2½ pints) water

230 g can of chopped tomatoes

2 fresh green chillies, chopped very finely

2 teaspoons salt, or to taste

¼ teaspoon ground turmeric

½ teaspoon freeze-dried ginger

1 teaspoon chilli powder

2 tablespoons lemon juice

2 tablespoons soft brown sugar

a knob of butter

15 g packet of fresh coriander, chopped finely, to garnish

For the tarka:

1 tablespoon sunflower or corn oil

2.5 cm (1-inch) cinnamon stick

4 cloves

1 teaspoon black mustard seeds

¼ teaspoon cumin seeds

½ teaspoon chilli powder

6–8 curry leaves (optional)

❶ Soak the lentils in hot water to cover for 10 minutes. Rinse the lentils with warm water and drain them.

❷ Add the measured water to the lentils in a large, heavy-based saucepan and bring to the boil over a high heat.

❸ Reduce the heat and simmer for 20 minutes; check that the lentils are well cooked at the end of this period.

❹ Liquidise the cooked lentils using a blender or an electric whisk. Add the tomatoes, chillies, salt, turmeric, ginger, chilli powder, lemon juice and sugar.

❺ Return to the heat and allow to simmer.

❻ Meanwhile, prepare the *tarka*. Heat the oil in a small pan. Add the remaining ingredients and stir for 1 minute over a low heat.

❼ Remove the *tarka* from the heat and stir it into the simmering dhal. Add the butter.

❽ Garnish with the chopped fresh coriander before serving.

Spinach and Dhal

Preparation and cooking time: 25 minutes.
Freezing: not recommended. Serves 2–3.

This is my sneaky short-cut to an authentic Indian dish. The slightly undercooked onions contrast beautifully with the smooth texture of the ready-prepared dhal. You can use any vegetables with this dhal when an unexpected guest arrives. I usually serve it with naan bread (which is always in my freezer for emergencies) and natural yogurt.

2 tablespoons corn or vegetable oil

1 large onion, sliced finely

5 cm (2-inch) cinnamon stick, broken

½ teaspoon garlic purée

½ teaspoon freeze-dried ginger

1 fresh green chilli, chopped very finely

230 g can of chopped tomatoes

¾ teaspoon salt, or to taste

¼ teaspoon ground turmeric

½ teaspoon ground cumin

½ teaspoon ground coriander

250 g (8 oz) frozen leaf spinach

400 g can of lentil dhal

15 g packet of fresh coriander, chopped finely

❶ Heat the oil in a medium-size saucepan over a medium heat. Add the onion, cinnamon pieces, garlic purée, ginger, and chilli, and stir-fry for 2–3 minutes.

❷ Add the tomatoes and stir in the salt, turmeric, cumin and coriander, and cook for a further 2–3 minutes.

❸ Add the spinach, cover and cook for 5 minutes.

❹ Add the dhal and coriander, cover and cook over a low heat for 5–10 minutes. Stir half-way through cooking.

Okra Curry

Preparation and cooking time: 25 minutes.
Freezing: recommended. Serves 3–4.

Okra, sometimes called 'ladies fingers', is an unusual vegetable with a sticky texture. In this recipe, the okra are stir-fried before being curried, since this reduces the stickiness. They are delicious with Chapatis (page 72), and Cucumber Raita (page 74).

500 g (1 lb) okra, topped and tailed
7 tablespoons olive oil
½ teaspoon salt, or to taste
1 tablespoon lemon juice
230 g can of chopped tomatoes
2 fresh green chillies, chopped very finely
1 teaspoon quick-frozen garlic

½ teaspoon freeze-dried ginger
½ teaspoon hot curry paste (optional)
1 teaspoon garam masala
½ teaspoon ground coriander
½ teaspoon ground cumin
15 g packet of fresh coriander, chopped finely

❶ Cut the okra into 1 cm (½-inch) pieces.
❷ Heat the oil in a large, lidded frying-pan or wok over a high heat. Gently fry the okra, with the salt and lemon juice, for 3–5 minutes.
❸ Cover and cook over a medium heat for a further 10 minutes, stirring occasionally.

❹ Remove the okra with a slotted spoon and let them drain on kitchen paper.
❺ Put all the other ingredients into the pan and stir well. Cook for 2 minutes.
❻ Return the okra to the pan, cover and cook over a medium heat for 5 minutes.

Potato and Cauliflower Curry

Preparation time: 10 minutes + 30 minutes cooking.
Freezing: not recommended. Serves 4.

2 tablespoons sunflower oil

½ teaspoon cumin seeds

4 ripe tomatoes, skinned and chopped, or a
    230 g can of chopped tomatoes

3 tablespoons passata (sieved tomatoes)

½ teaspoon ground turmeric

1 teaspoon ground coriander

½ teaspoon ground cumin

1 teaspoon chilli powder

500 g (1 lb) cauliflower, cut into small florets

500 g (1 lb) potatoes, peeled and cut into
small cubes

1 teaspoon salt, or to taste

1 teaspoon garam masala

2 green chillies, de-seeded and sliced
lengthways, to garnish

❶ Preheat the oven to Gas Mark 6/200°C/400°F.

❷ Heat the oil in a flameproof casserole dish with a tight-fitting lid. Remove from the heat and stir in the cumin seeds.

❸ Add the tomatoes, passata, turmeric, coriander, cumin and chilli powder. Cook for 5 minutes.

❹ Add the vegetables, with the salt, to the casserole dish. Stir well.

❺ Cover and bake in the oven for around 30 minutes, or until the potatoes are cooked.

❻ Remove from the oven and gently fold in the garam masala. Serve garnished with the green chillies.

Fifteen-Minute Dhal

Preparation and cooking time: 15 minutes.
Freezing: not recommended. Serves 4.

My secret short-cut to an authentic dish which, if cooked traditionally, can take up to an hour. Serve with boiled rice and salad.

2 × 432 g can of yellow split-peas

1 tablespoon vegetable or corn oil

6 curry leaves (optional)

½ teaspoon black mustard seeds

½ teaspoon cumin seeds

2 cloves

2 fresh green chillies, chopped very finely

1 teaspoon quick-frozen garlic

100 g (3½ oz) passata (sieved tomatoes)

1 teaspoon salt, or to taste

½ teaspoon ground cumin

375 ml (12 fl oz) hot water

1 tablespoon lemon juice

1 heaped tablespoon tamarind and date pickle
    (optional)

2 × 15 g packet of fresh coriander, chopped

❶ Purée the split-peas in a blender or with a potato masher.

❷ Heat the oil in a large saucepan over a medium heat. Add the curry leaves (if used) and the mustard seeds. Cover and allow the seeds to pop for a few seconds.

❸ Add the cumin seeds, cloves, chillies and garlic, and stir-fry for 1 minute.

❹ Add the passata, salt and cumin and stir well.

❺ Add the puréed split peas and the water. Cook, covered, for 5 minutes.

❻ Stir in the lemon juice, tamarind and date pickle and chopped fresh coriander.

Black-Eyed Beans with Coconut and Lemon

Preparation and cooking time: 15 minutes.
Freezing: not recommended. Serves 4.

A speedy and nutritious dish that can be made with any canned beans or lentils. Serve with Chapatis (page 72) and Cucumber Raita (page 74).

2 tablespoons olive oil

1 teaspoon black mustard seeds

1 teaspoon quick-frozen garlic

½ teaspoon freeze-dried ginger

2 fresh green chillies, chopped very finely

250 g (8 oz) passata (sieved tomatoes)

½ teaspoon salt, or to taste

1 teaspoon ground turmeric

1 teaspoon ground cumin

1 teaspoon ground coriander

1 heaped teaspoon hot curry paste

4 tablespoons desiccated coconut

2 tablespoons lemon juice

1 teaspoon garam masala

15 g packet of fresh coriander, chopped

150 ml (¼ pint) hot water

2 × 432 g can of black-eyed beans, drained

❶ Heat the oil in a large saucepan. Reduce heat, add the mustard seeds, cover and allow the seeds to pop for a few seconds.
❷ Add the garlic, ginger, chillies and passata. Simmer for 2–3 minutes.

❸ Add all the other main ingredients and stir well. Cover and cook over a medium heat for 5 minutes.
Variation: Omit the coconut and lemon for a simple bean curry.

Stuffed Aubergines

Preparation time: 15 minutes + 30 minutes cooking.
Freezing: recommended. Serves 4.

1 kg (2 lb) small aubergines

2 tablespoons sunflower oil

1 teaspoon black mustard seeds

150 ml (¼ pint) water

For the paste:

100 g (3½ oz) raw peanuts, chopped or ground coarsely

2 tablespoons desiccated coconut

75 g (3 oz) tomato purée

¼ teaspoon ground turmeric

2 teaspoons ground coriander

1 teaspoon ground cumin

1 teaspoon chilli powder

1 teaspoon sugar

1 teaspoon salt, or to taste

15 g packet of fresh coriander, chopped finely

❶ Preheat the oven to Gas Mark 6/200°C/400°F.
❷ Make a slit along the length of each aubergine by cutting through the pulp. Be careful not to cut it completely into two pieces.
❸ Mix all the paste ingredients together and stuff each aubergine slit with paste.
❹ Heat the oil in a large flameproof casserole dish. Fry the mustard seeds until they begin to pop.
❺ Add the stuffed aubergines, water and any leftover paste. Cover with a tight-fitting lid and bake in the oven for 30 minutes.

Stuffed Banana Curry

Preparation and cooking time: 35 minutes.
Freezing: not recommended. Serves 4.

An unusual sweet-and-sour dish, where the sweetness comes naturally from the bananas. You will need a large, non-stick frying-pan with a lid. Be careful not to break the bananas when transferring them from the pan to the serving dish.

Suggested accompaniments include naan bread or Chapatis (page 72), with natural yogurt and salad. Remember to tell your fellow diners not to eat the banana skins!

6 bananas, unpeeled, washed and halved
    crossways
1½ tablespoons vegetable or corn oil
1 teaspoon black mustard seeds
100 g (3½ oz) passata (sieved tomatoes)
1 teaspoon ground cumin
1 teaspoon ground coriander
½ teaspoon ground turmeric
½ teaspoon freeze-dried ginger
½ teaspoon quick-frozen garlic
2 fresh green chillies, chopped very finely
5 tablespoons hot water

For the stuffing:
2 heaped teaspoons ground cumin
2 heaped teaspoons ground coriander
1 teaspoon ground turmeric
1–2 teaspoons chilli powder, or to taste
1 teaspoon tomato purée
1 teaspoon garam masala
2 tablespoons water
2 tablespoons lemon juice
1 tablespoon oil
15 g packet of fresh coriander, chopped finely
1 teaspoon salt, or to taste

❶ Make a slit along each banana half, making sure not to cut the banana completely in two.

❷ Mix all the stuffing ingredients together. Gently stuff each banana half with about 1 teaspoon of the filling.

❸ Heat the oil on a medium heat and add the black mustard seeds. Allow the seeds to pop for a few seconds.

❹ Add the passata, cumin, coriander, turmeric, ginger, garlic and chillies. Cook for 1 minute.

❺ Add the water and stir.

❻ Place the bananas in the frying-pan, packing them well in so that all the bananas are in one layer. Cover and cook over a medium heat for 5 minutes.

❼ Reduce the heat to low, and add a few tablespoons of hot water ifs are sticking to the bottom of the pan. The banana skins will start to turn black.turn black.

❽ Cook for a further 5–10 minutes on a low heat. Serve immediately.

Masala Potatoes

Preparation and cooking time: 10 minutes.
Freezing: not recommended. Serves 4.

2 tablespoons vegetable or corn oil
1 teaspoon black mustard seeds
1 teaspoon cumin seeds
150 g (5 oz) passata (sieved tomatoes)
1 tablespoon tomato purée
1½ teaspoons salt, or to taste
1 teaspoon ground turmeric
2 teaspoons chilli powder, or to taste
1 teaspoon ground cumin

1 teaspoon dried mint
2 tablespoons crispy topping onions
820 g can of potatoes
150 ml (¼ pint) hot water
2 tablespoons lemon juice
15 g packet of fresh coriander, chopped
   roughly
½ teaspoon garam masala
sliced spring onions, to garnish

❶ Heat the oil in a large saucepan. Add the mustard seeds, cover and allow to pop over a low heat for a few seconds.
❷ Off the heat, add the cumin seeds.
❸ Return the pan to the heat and add the passata, tomato purée, salt, turmeric, chilli powder, cumin, mint and crispy topping onions. Cook over a medium heat for 2 minutes.
❹ Add the potatoes, water and lemon juice. Cover and cook over a medium heat for 5 minutes.
❺ Stir in the chopped coriander and the garam masala. Garnish and serve.

Special Vegetable Rice

Preparation time: 15 minutes + 20 minutes cooking.
Freezing: not recommended. Serves 2–3.

This recipe makes use of a pack of frozen special mixed vegetables.

250 g (8 oz) basmati rice
5 tablespoons vegetable or corn oil
1 large onion, sliced
4 × 5 cm (2-inch) cinnamon stick, broken
6 cloves
6 black peppercorns
2 cardamom pods
2 teaspoons cumin seeds
1 teaspoon fennel seeds (optional)

500 g (1 lb) frozen special mixed vegetables
2½ teaspoons salt, or to taste
2 teaspoons freeze-dried ginger
2 teaspoons quick-frozen garlic
3 fresh green chillies, chopped very finely
chilli powder (optional)
½ teaspoon ground turmeric
500 ml (18 fl oz) boiling water

❶ Rinse the rice and soak it in plenty of cold water.
❷ Heat the oil in a heavy frying-pan with a tight-fitting lid. Add the onion, cinnamon pieces, cloves, peppercorns, cardamoms, cumin seeds and fennel seeds (if used). Fry gently for 2 minutes.
❸ Stir in the vegetables, salt, ginger, garlic, chillies, chilli powder (if used) and turmeric. Stir-fry for 3–5 minutes.
❹ Add the water and bring to the boil.
❺ Drain the rice, stir it into the pan and cover with a tight-fitting lid. Cook over a medium heat for 20 minutes.

Crispy Cabbage Curry
Preparation and cooking time: 20 minutes.
Freezing: not recommended. Serves 3–4.

I had hated cabbage ever since school meals, but this dish certainly put a stop to that. A lightly spiced curry which goes well with natural yogurt and naan bread or Chapatis (page 72).

2½ tablespoons vegetable or corn oil
1 teaspoon black mustard seeds
½ teaspoon caraway seeds (optional)
1 teaspoon quick-frozen garlic
½ teaspoon freeze-dried ginger
2 fresh green chillies, chopped very finely
2 × 5 cm (2-inch) cinnamon stick, broken
1 small white cabbage, weighing about 750 g
    (1½ lb), shredded finely

125 g (4 oz) frozen petits pois
3 tomatoes, chopped finely
1½ teaspoons salt, or to taste
1 teaspoon ground cumin
½ teaspoon ground coriander
½ teaspoon ground turmeric
15 g packet of fresh coriander, chopped
½ teaspoon garam masala
chilli powder, to taste (optional)

❶ Heat the oil over a low heat. Add the mustard seeds and the caraway seeds (if using), and allow them to pop for a few seconds.
❷ Stir in the garlic, ginger, chillies and cinnamon pieces.

❸ Add the cabbage, peas, tomatoes and salt. Stir well, cover and cook for 5 minutes.
❹ Add all the other ingredients. Stir thoroughly. Cover and cook for a further 5 minutes, or until the vegetables are just tender.

'All-in-the-Pot' Dishes

In these recipes, the ingredients are placed in the pot all at once; the aroma and flavour develop whilst you have time to set the table or prepare accompaniments. A great short-cut to standard Indian cooking.

Prawns and Sweetcorn in Coconut Cream

Preparation time: 10 minutes + 10 minutes cooking.
Freezing: not recommended. Serves 3–4.

Creamed coconut is sold in 200 g (7 oz) blocks. You can also buy powdered coconut milk in a box, or canned coconut milk. Serve with rice or as a warming main-meal soup with french bread.

400 g (13 oz) frozen peeled prawns

340 g can of sweetcorn and peppers

2 heaped tablespoons crispy topping onions

1 tablespoon corn oil

75 g (3 oz) creamed coconut, chopped, or 4 tablespoons coconut milk powder, made up with water as directed, or 200 ml (7 fl oz) coconut milk

2 fresh tomatoes, chopped

15 g packet of fresh coriander, chopped

1 teaspoon lemon juice

1 teaspoon freeze-dried ginger

2 teaspoons garlic purée

2 fresh green chillies, chopped very finely

½ teaspoon salt, or to taste

¼ teaspoon ground turmeric

1 teaspoon red chilli powder

100 ml (3½ fl oz) hot water

garam masala, to garnish

❶ Put all the ingredients into a large non-stick saucepan and stir well. Cover with a tight-fitting lid, and cook for 10 minutes over a medium heat.

❷ Garnish and serve.

Kheema Peas

Preparation time: 10 minutes + 35 minutes cooking.
Freezing: recommended, without the frozen peas. Serves 4.

For this recipe, you do not strictly need oil for frying, because the minced beef produces some. So make this dish healthier by omitting the oil altogether. Serve with Chapatis (page 72), naan bread or boiled rice.

750 g (1½ lb) lean minced beef

2 tablespoons oil

300 g (10 oz) chopped tomatoes

2 teaspoons freeze-dried ginger

2 teaspoons quick-frozen garlic

3 fresh green chillies, chopped very finely

1 teaspoon chilli powder, or to taste

1 large onion, sliced

1 teaspoon ground cumin

1 teaspoon ground coriander

½ teaspoon garam masala, plus extra to garnish

2 teaspoons salt, or to taste

75 g (3 oz) cashew nuts, plus extra to garnish (optional)

2 × 5 cm (2-inch) cinnamon stick

2 cardamom pods

6 black peppercorns

½ teaspoon ground black pepper

4 cloves

150 ml (¼ pint) water

¼ teaspoon ground turmeric

250 g (8 oz) frozen peas

2 × 15 g packet of fresh coriander, chopped

❶ Heat a heavy-based pan over a high heat and add all the ingredients except the peas and coriander, starting with the minced beef. Blend the ingredients together thoroughly.

❷ Cover and cook over a medium heat for 20 minutes.

❸ Add the peas and coriander. Stir well, cover and cook for a further 15 minutes. Garnish and serve

Baked Fish in Yogurt and Lemon

Preparation time: 15 minutes + 20 minutes cooking.
Freezing: not recommended. Serves 4.

A healthy fish-dish that goes particularly well with Rice with Shredded Vegetables and Caraway Seeds (page 68).

1 large onion, sliced thinly into rings
4 large frozen haddock fillets, weighing about
    625 g (1½ lb), each cut into 3
For the yogurt sauce:
200 g (7 oz) natural yogurt
2 tablespoons olive oil
1 teaspoon quick-frozen garlic
2 fresh green chillies, chopped very finely

juice of a small lemon (reserve 1 or 2 slices
    for garnish)
1 teaspoon salt
15 g packet of fresh coriander, chopped finely
1 teaspoon curry powder
For the topping:
1 green pepper, cut into rings and de-seeded
1 large tomato, sliced

❶ Preheat the oven to Gas Mark 6/200°C/400°F. Grease a large, shallow ovenproof dish well with olive oil.
❷ Line the dish with a layer of onion rings, and then add the fish in one layer.
❸ Mix the sauce ingredients together and then coat the fish well with sauce.
❹ Bake in the oven for 15 minutes
❺ Remove the fish, baste it and top it with the peppers and tomatoes. Return it to the oven for 5 minutes and then serve immediately.

Chicken Korma with Cashew Nuts

Preparation time: 10 minutes + 30 minutes cooking.
Freezing: not recommended. Serves 4.

A thick, creamy dish that goes particularly well with plain boiled rice. The contrasting texture of the cashew nuts adds interest.

1 tablespoon olive oil
2 × 5 cm (2-inch) cinnamon stick, broken
8 chicken portions on the bone (e.g. thighs or
    drumsticks)
4 fresh green chillies, chopped very finely
½ teaspoon freeze-dried ginger
½ teaspoon quick-frozen garlic

335 g jar of korma cooking sauce
3 tablespoons crispy topping onions
2 teaspoons ground cumin
50 g (2 oz) cashew nuts, broken
½ teaspoon salt, or to taste
100 ml (3½ fl oz) hot water
2 × 15 g packet of fresh coriander, chopped

❶ Heat the pan and add all the ingredients in the order in which they appear in the list, stirring after every few additions.
❷ Cover and cook over a medium heat for 30 minutes, or until the chicken is fully cooked.
❸ Stir every 5–10 minutes and add a few tablespoons of hot water each time if the sauce is becoming too thick.

Beef Curry

Preparation time: 10 minutes + 20 minutes cooking.
Freezing: recommended. Serves 4.

This is a quick and easy method of preparation for this popular dish. You can use leg or shoulder of lamb, if you prefer this to rump steak.

3 tablespoons vegetable or corn oil

1 teaspoon freeze-dried ginger

1 teaspoon quick-frozen garlic

2 fresh green chillies, chopped very finely

2 cardamom pods

6 black peppercorns

5 cm (2-inch) cinnamon stick, broken

1 teaspoon ground turmeric

1 teaspoon ground cumin

1 heaped teaspoon hot curry paste

1 teaspoon ground coriander

1 teaspoon salt, or to taste

750 g (1½ lb) rump steak, cut into 2.5 cm (1-inch) cubes

100 g (3½ oz) passata (sieved tomatoes)

1 tablespoon tomato purée

3 tablespoons crispy topping onions

125 ml (4 fl oz) hot water

chilli powder (optional)

15 g packet of fresh coriander, chopped

1 teaspoon garam masala

❶ Heat a heavy-based pan. Maintain on a medium heat whilst adding the ingredients in the order in which they appear on the list.

❷ Stir well after every few additions, and especially well after adding the meat.

❸ Cover and cook over a medium heat until the steak is tender (around 20 minutes).

❹ Half-way through cooking, add some more hot water to dilute. Stir and continue to cook.

❺ Stir in the fresh coriander and the garam masala.

Variation: To make a beef curry with dhal, simply add a 420 g can of lentil dhal to the cooked beef curry and heat through.

Thick Chicken Masala

Preparation and cooking time: 40 minutes.
Freezing: recommended. Serves 4.

The flavour of this dish develops best if small amounts of water are added at a time. If you find that doing this every 5 minutes is too cumbersome, double the amount of water and stir every 10 minutes. Reduce the cooking time somewhat if boneless chicken is used.

1–2 tablespoons olive oil
4 onions, chopped finely
1 teaspoon quick-frozen garlic
3 fresh green chillies, chopped very finely
8 chicken portions on the bone (e.g. thighs or drumsticks)
3 tablespoons tomato purée
¾ teaspoon salt, or to taste

¾ teaspoon coarsely ground black pepper, or to taste
1 teaspoon garam masala
4 teaspoons curry powder
2 × 15 g packet of fresh coriander, chopped roughly
150 ml (¼ pint) hot water

❶ Heat a heavy-based non-stick pan. Put all the ingredients into the pan in the order in which they appear in the ingredients list.

❷ Stir after every few additions, particularly after adding the chicken.

❸ Cover and cook over a medium heat until the chicken is fully cooked (about 30 minutes). Add 4 tablespoons of hot water after each 5 minutes, stirring well.

Minced Beef with Fenugreek and Spinach

**Preparation time: 15 minutes + 20 minutes cooking.
Freezing: recommended after step 2. Serves 4.**

If you use chopped spinach for this dish, you will need to watch out for the whole spices (especially the peppercorns), since they are less visible amongst the spinach. Try not to break the cinnamon sticks into very small pieces, since these can also get mixed into the spinach. Serve with naan bread, Cucumber Raita (page 74) or boiled rice.

3 tablespoons vegetable or corn oil

1 large onion, chopped

½ teaspoon freeze-dried ginger

1 teaspoon quick-frozen garlic

3 fresh green chillies, chopped very finely

1 teaspoon fennel seeds (optional)

5 cm (2-inch) cinnamon stick, broken

2 cardamom pods

6 cloves

6 black peppercorns

¾ teaspoon ground fenugreek

500 g (1 lb) lean minced beef

1 teaspoon ground turmeric

1 teaspoon ground coriander

1 teaspoon ground cumin

1½ teaspoons salt, or to taste

150 g (5 oz) passata (sieved tomatoes)

1 teaspoon tomato purée

100 ml (3½ fl oz) hot water

100 g (3½ oz) frozen leaf or chopped spinach

15 g packet of fresh coriander, chopped

1 teaspoon garam masala

❶ Heat a heavy-based non-stick pan. Add the ingredients in the order in which they appear on the list except the spinach, fresh coriander and garam masala. Stir after every few additions, especially after adding the minced beef.

❷ Cover and cook over a medium heat, stirring occasionally, for 20 minutes.

❸ Stir in the spinach, coriander and garam masala. Cover and cook for 5 minutes.

Side Dishes

Side dishes such as cooling raita, tangy chutneys, rice and breads really enhance the pleasure of Indian food. These are so simple and quick to make that you will find it easy to add them to your midweek repertoire.

Rice with Shredded Vegetables and Caraway Seeds

Preparation time: 15 minutes + 20 minutes cooking.
Freezing: recommended. Serves 6.

A mild and colourful dish that goes well with fish or dhal dishes. It can be served on its own with relish, Cucumber Raita (page 74) and salad if desired. You will need a large heavy-based pan with a tight-fitting lid.

500 g (1 lb) basmati rice

4 tablespoons corn or vegetable oil

2 teaspoons cumin seeds

1½ teaspoons caraway seeds

2 large onions, sliced

3 cardamom pods

6 black peppercorns

6 cloves

2 × 5 cm (2-inch) cinnamon stick, broken

2 teaspoons garlic purée

2 teaspoons freeze-dried ginger

4 fresh green chillies, chopped very finely

1 litre (1¾ pints) hot water

3 tablespoons hoisin sauce

2 teaspoons salt, or to taste

juice of ½ lemon or 3 teaspoons lemon juice

1 small white cabbage, weighing about 500 g (1 lb), shredded or grated

375 g (12 oz) carrots, shredded or grated

❶ Rinse the rice well and put it to soak in plenty of cold water.

❷ Heat the oil. Remove the pan from the heat, add the cumin and caraway seeds and wait till they crackle. Immediately add the onions, cardamoms, peppercorns, cloves and cinnamon pieces.

❸ Stir in the garlic purée, ginger and chillies. Fry gently for 2 minutes.

❹ Add the hot water, hoisin sauce, salt and lemon juice.

❺ Add the vegetables and drained rice to the pan, taking care not to break the rice up whilst stirring.

❻ Cover with a tight-fitting lid and cook over a medium heat for 15–20 minutes.

Jeera Potatoes

Preparation and cooking time: 30 minutes.
Freezing: not recommended. Serves 4–6.

A dish that uses freshly ground black pepper to impart a different type
of hot flavour from chilli powder. For best results, add the water a little
at a time during cooking, as the recipe instructs. Serve with Red Lentil
Dhal with Tarka (page 40), Chapatis (page 72) and Cucumber Raita
(page 74), or as a snack on toast.

4 tablespoons vegetable or corn oil

1 cinnamon stick, broken

3 cloves

4 curry leaves (optional)

¼ teaspoon onion seeds (optional)

2 teaspoons cumin seeds

½ teaspoon coriander seeds

½ teaspoon quick-frozen garlic

¾ teaspoon freeze-dried ginger

2 fresh green chillies, de-seeded and chopped
finely

750 g (1½ lb) potatoes, peeled or scrubbed
and sliced thinly

1 teaspoon ground turmeric

½ teaspoon ground cumin

½ teaspoon ground coriander

1½ teaspoons salt, or to taste

200 ml (7 fl oz) hot water

2 × 15 g packet of fresh coriander, chopped

1 tablespoon lemon juice

½ teaspoon freshly ground black pepper, or to
taste

chopped spring onions, to garnish

❶ Heat the oil in a large pan, remove the
pan from the heat and add the cinnamon
pieces, cloves, curry leaves (if using),
onion seeds (if using), cumin seeds and
coriander seeds.

❷ Return to a low heat and add the
garlic, ginger and chillies. Stir-fry for 1
minute.

❸ Add the potatoes, turmeric, cumin,
coriander and salt and stir-fry for

5 minutes over a medium heat.

❹ Add 100 ml (3½ fl oz) of the hot
water. Stir and simmer for 5 minutes.

❺ Stir in the remaining 100 ml (3½ fl oz)
of water. Cover and cook for 5 minutes, or
until the potatoes are cooked. (Add more
water if necessary.)

❻ Add the chopped fresh coriander,
lemon juice and black pepper. Garnish
and serve.

Chapatis

Preparation and cooking time: 40 minutes.
Freezing: recommended. Makes 10.

Chapatis (or rotis) are the main accompaniment to most Indian dishes. The dedicated lady of the house traditionally cooked fresh chapatis and served them hot off the stove whilst her family began the meal. This practice is still common, although lack of time often means that chapatis need to be prepared in advance. In the Asian household, they are rolled out using a special slim rolling pin and a round board. They are then cooked on a shallow, curved clay pan for even roasting. You can use ordinary rolling utensils and a frying-pan instead.

Hot chapatis can be served with a variety of dishes. The dough and the cooked chapatis can be stored in the freezer. I often defrost chapatis directly over my gas hob, holding them in tongs or a rack, although grilling is just as good.

300 g (10 oz) plain wholemeal or white flour
½ teaspoon salt, or to taste
2 tablespoons sunflower or corn oil

150 ml (¼ pint) warm water
50 g (2 oz) plain white flour, for rolling

❶ Sift the flour and the salt together. Add the oil and mix well.

❷ Gradually add the water, mixing continuously until a soft dough is formed.

❸ Knead for 3–5 minutes until the dough is no longer sticky.

❹ Divide the ball of dough into 10 pieces and flour each piece on both sides using the plain flour.

❺ Roll out each ball into an 18 cm (7–inch) round, lifting the round gently as you work. If it begins to stick to the rolling pin, flour again on both sides and resume rolling.

❻ Heat a frying-pan on the highest setting on the hob and place the rolled chapati on it. Turn the chapati over when brown specks begin to appear on the underside. Cook the second side of the chapati.

❼ Flip the chapati over again. Use a clean ball of kitchen paper or a tea towel to press the chapati all over, to circulate the steam.

❽ Remove and serve hot. The chapatis can be stacked in a pile and kept warm, wrapped in aluminium foil.

Cucumber Raita

Preparation time: 5 minutes.
Freezing: not recommended. Serves 4.

2 × 150 g (5 oz) carton of natural yogurt

2 spring onions (green stems only), sliced thinly

10 cm (4-inch) piece of cucumber, diced

1 teaspoon ground cumin

coarsely ground black pepper, to taste (optional)

15 g packet of fresh coriander, chopped finely

a pinch of salt

❶ Mix all the ingredients together. Serve lightly chilled.

Tamarind Sauce

Preparation time: 5 minutes. Freezing: recommended. Serves 4.

This is excellent with Chilli and Herb Chicken Wings (page 6), Eastern Fried Chicken (page 36) or any kebabs.

3 tablespoons tamarind and date pickle

100 ml (3½ fl oz) water

1 spring onion, chopped finely

1 tablespoon lemon juice

½ teaspoon chilli powder, or to taste

15 g packet of fresh coriander, chopped finely

❶ Combine all the ingredients and stir thoroughly.

Tomato and Onion Salad

Preparation time: 15 minutes.
Freezing: not recommended. Serves 6.

1 kg (2 lb) fresh tomatoes, chopped

3 onions, grated coarsely

1 teaspoon salt, or to taste

½ teaspoon chilli powder

1 tablespoon lemon juice

15 g packet of fresh coriander, chopped

❶ Mix together the tomatoes and onions.

❷ Add the salt, chilli powder, lemon juice and a tablespoon of chopped coriander. Toss gently.

❸ Serve garnished with the remaining chopped fresh coriander.

Mushrooms in Hot Sauce

Preparation and cooking time: 10 minutes.
Freezing: recommended. Serves 4.

2 tablespoons olive oil

25 g (1 oz) butter

1 teaspoon quick-frozen garlic

½ teaspoon garlic grain pepper

625 g (1¼ lb) button mushrooms

¾ teaspoon curry powder

¼ teaspoon salt, or to taste

15 g packet of fresh coriander, chopped

2 teaspoons lemon juice (optional)

❶ Heat the oil in a wok or frying-pan and melt in the butter in it.

❷ Add the garlic, garlic grain pepper, mushrooms, curry powder and salt. Fry gently for 4 minutes.

❸ Stir in the chopped fresh coriander and lemon juice, if used. Serve immediately.

Sautéd Okra with Cumin Seeds

Preparation time: 10 minutes + 30 minutes cooking.
Freezing: recommended. Serves 4.

This is an exotic side-dish that complements many dhal and rice dishes. The whole okra can be beautifully presented in a star shape for entertaining.

3 tablespoons vegetable or olive oil

½ teaspoon quick-frozen garlic

½ teaspoon freeze-dried ginger

2 fresh green chillies, chopped very finely

1 heaped teaspoon cumin seeds

500 g (1 lb) okra, topped and tailed

1 teaspoon ground turmeric

½ teaspoon salt, or to taste

❶ Heat the oil in a large frying-pan or wok. Add the garlic, ginger and chillies.

❷ Remove the frying-pan from the heat and add the cumin seeds. Stir the seeds in quickly to prevent them from burning.

❸ Return to the heat and add all the other ingredients.

❹ Cook, uncovered, for 20–30 minutes, stirring occasionally. If the okra begin to stick, add 150 ml (¼ pint) hot water and continue cooking, uncovered. The liquid should almost all have evaporated by the end.

Sweetcorn in Mustard Seeds and Lemon

Preparation and cooking time: 20 minutes.
Freezing: recommended. Serves 3.

1½ tablespoons vegetable or corn oil

1 teaspoon black mustard seeds

1 teaspoon cumin seeds

¼ teaspoon quick-frozen garlic

¼ teaspoon freeze-dried ginger

1–2 fresh green chillies, chopped very finely

125 g (4 oz) canned chopped tomatoes

½ teaspoon ground turmeric

½ teaspoon ground cumin

½ teaspoon ground coriander

¼ teaspoon salt, or to taste

326 g can of sweetcorn

125 ml (4 fl oz) hot water

¼ teaspoon garam masala

2 tablespoons lemon juice

2 × 15 g packet of fresh coriander, chopped

❶ Heat the oil in a pan. Reduce the heat and add the mustard seeds. Cover immediately, and wait until the seeds have stopped crackling.

❷ Add the cumin seeds.

❸ Add the garlic, ginger and chillies and stir well.

❹ Add the tomatoes, turmeric, cumin, coriander and salt. Allow to simmer for 3–5 minutes, stirring occasionally.

❺ Add the sweetcorn, water, garam masala, lemon juice and chopped fresh coriander. Cover and cook for 5–10 minutes.

Chilli Chips

Preparation and cooking time: 15 minutes.
Freezing: not recommended. Serves 4.

2 tablespoons olive oil

1 teaspoon quick-frozen garlic

1 kg (2 lb) 5%-fat oven chips

½ teaspoon Cajun seasoning, herb pepper or dill pepper

2 teaspoons piri-piri seasoning

¾ teaspoon dried oregano

½–1 teaspoon salt, to taste

½ teaspoon garlic grain pepper

To garnish:

chilli powder

lemon wedges

❶ Heat the oil in a large non-stick wok or frying-pan. Add the garlic and stir-fry for a few seconds.

❷ Add all the other ingredients and fry gently over a high heat until the chips are browned and cooked (10–15 minutes).

❸ Place the chips in a serving dish and sprinkle with chilli powder, as desired. Garnish and serve.

Index